Contents

Cherry Lane Music Company
Director of Publications/Project Editor: Mark Phillips
Project Coordinator: Rebecca Skidmore

ISBN 978-1-60378-045-2

Visit our website at www.cherrylaneprint.com

Abide with Me

Words by Henry F. Lyte
Music by William H. Monk

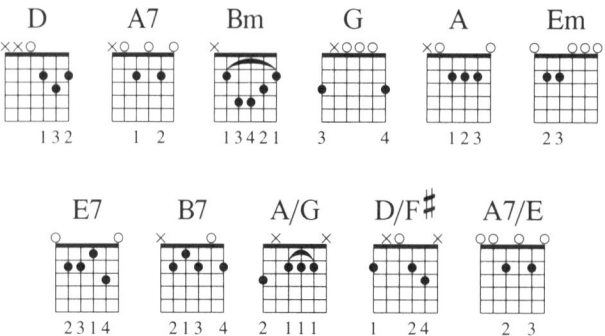

Verse 1

D   A7 |Bm   D |G   A |D |
A - bide with me. Fast falls the even - tide.

D   G   D |G   D |Em   A   D   E7|A |
The dark - ness deep - ens, Lord with me a - bide.

D   A7 |Bm   D |G   B7 |Em |
When other help - ers fail and comforts flee,

A/G   D/F♯   A7/E |D   A7   Bm   Em |D/A   A   A7 |D   ‖
Help of the help - less, oh, a - bide with me.

Verse 2

D   A7 |Bm   D |G   A |D |
Swift to its close ebbs out life's little day.

D   G   D |G   D |Em   A   D   E7|A |
Earth's joys grow dim, its glor - ies pass a - way.

D   A7 |Bm   D |G   B7 |Em |
Change and de - cay in all a - round I see.

A/G   D/F♯   A7/E |D   A7   Bm   Em |D/A   A   A7 |D   ‖
O Thou, who chang - est not, a - bide with me.

Verse 3

```
D  A7      |Bm  D  |G   A       |D              |
```
I need Thy pre - sence ev - 'ry passing hour.
```
D    G    D |G    D |Em  A  D   E7 |A           |
```
What but Thy grace can foil the tempt - er's power?
```
D     A7     |Bm  D |G          B7   |Em           |
```
Who, like Thy - self, my guide and stay can be?
```
A/G       D/F♯ A7/E|D    A7    Bm  Em |D/A  A  A7 |D        ||
```
Through cloud and sun - shine, oh, a - bide with   me.

Verse 4

```
D    A7      |Bm  D |G   A       |D          |
```
Hold Thou Thy cross be - fore my closing eyes.
```
D    G      D |G    D |Em  A  D  E7 |A           |
```
Shine through the gloom and point me to the skies.
```
D       A7     |Bm   D |G          B7    |Em          |
```
Heav'n's morning breaks, and earth's vain shadows flee.
```
A/G D/F♯ A7/E |D    A7 Bm  Em |D/A  A  A7 |D        ||
```
In life, in   death, O Lord, a - bide with   me.

All Creatures of Our God and King

Words by Francis of Assisi
Translated by William Henry Draper
Music from Geistliche Kirchengesang

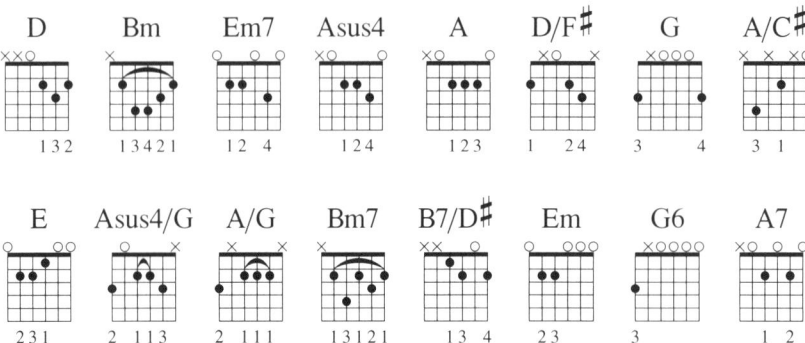

Verse 1

‖D   Bm Em7|Asus4 A
All creatures of our God and King,

D | Bm Em7|Asus4 A
Lift up your voice and with us sing.

D/F♯ |G D Bm A/C♯|D E A
Alle - lu - ia! Al - le - lu - ia!

D/F♯ |D   G |Asus4 A
Thou burning sun with gold - en beam,

D | G |D
Thou silver moon with soft - er gleam.

Refrain

G ‖Asus4/G A/G D/F♯
Alle - lu - ia!

Em7 D/F♯ |Asus4/G A Bm7
Al - le - lu - ia!

A/C♯ |D E A
Al - le - lu - ia!

Bm7 A/C♯ |D Em A/C♯ B7/D♯
Al - le - lu - ia!

Em D/F♯ |G6 A A7|D
Al - le - lu - ia!

Verse 2

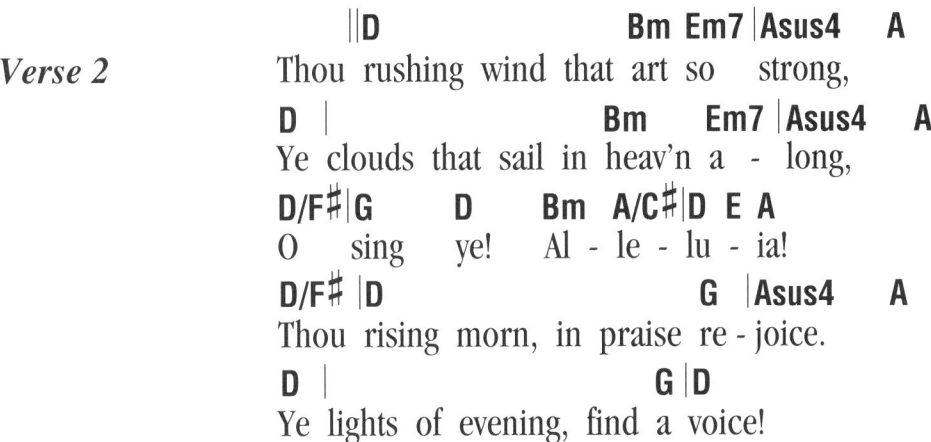

```
          ‖D                Bm  Em7 |Asus4    A
Thou  rushing  wind  that  art  so    strong,
          D  |                 Bm    Em7 |Asus4    A
Ye  clouds  that  sail  in  heav'n  a  -  long,
          D/F♯|G       D     Bm  A/C♯|D  E  A
O     sing     ye!   Al  -  le - lu - ia!
          D/F♯ |D                  G  |Asus4    A
Thou  rising  morn,  in  praise  re - joice.
          D  |                  G |D
Ye  lights  of  evening,  find  a  voice!
```

Repeat Refrain

Verse 3

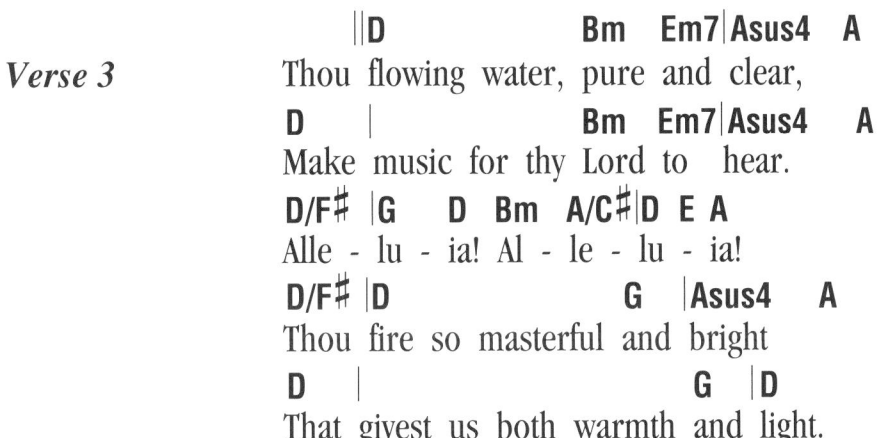

```
          ‖D             Bm   Em7 |Asus4  A
Thou  flowing  water,  pure  and  clear,
          D   |              Bm   Em7 |Asus4    A
Make  music  for  thy  Lord  to    hear.
          D/F♯ |G     D   Bm  A/C♯|D  E  A
Alle - lu - ia!  Al  -  le - lu - ia!
          D/F♯ |D                 G  |Asus4    A
Thou  fire  so  masterful  and  bright
          D   |                 G  |D
That  givest  us  both  warmth  and  light.
```

Repeat Refrain

All Things Bright and Beautiful

Words by Cecil Frances Alexander
17th Century English Melody

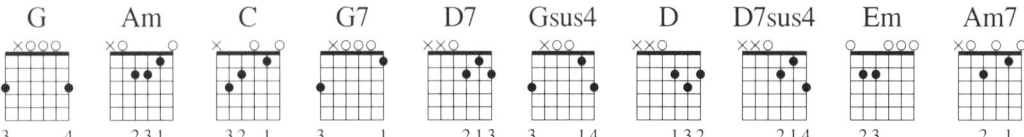

Refrain

G   Am   G |C   Am G
All things bright and beau - ti - ful,

G7|C   D7 |G   Gsus4 G |
All creatures great and small,

G G7   C   G |C   Am   G
All things wise and won - der - ful:

G7 |C   D7 |G   Gsus4 G
The Lord God made them all.

Verse 1

D ‖G G7 |C   Am
Each little flower that opens,

   |D D7 |G   Gsus4 G
Each little bird that sings,

D7sus4|G   Em |Am7 D7
God   made their glowing col - ors

 |G   C   D7 |G   Gsus4 G   ‖
And made their tiny wings.

Repeat Refrain

Verse 2

```
         D  ‖G       G7    |C          Am
The purple-headed mountains,
          |D     D7     |G Gsus4 G
The river running by,
D7sus4|G       Em     |Am7    D7
The     sunset and the morn - ing
          |G      C     D7   |G Gsus4 G         ‖
That bright - ens up the sky.
```

Repeat Refrain

Verse 3

```
         D  ‖G         G7    |C        Am
The cold wind in the winter,
          |D        D7     |G Gsus4 G
The pleasant summer sun,
D7sus4 |G         Em    |Am7  D7
The     ripe fruits in the gar - den:
          |G     C     D7    |G Gsus4 G         ‖
God made them, every one.
```

Repeat Refrain

Verse 4

```
         D  ‖G      G7     |C         Am
God gave us eyes to see them
          |D       D7       |G Gsus4 G
And lips that we might tell
D7sus4 |G        Em      |Am7   D7
How    great is God al - might - y,
          |G    C     D7   |G Gsus4 G         ‖
Who has made all things well.
```

Repeat Refrain

Amazing Grace

Words by John Newton
From A Collection of Sacred Ballads
Traditional American Melody
From Carrell and Clayton's Virginia Harmony

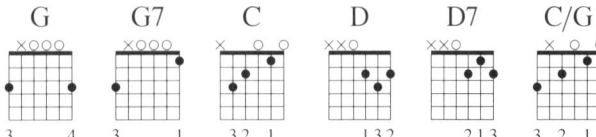

Verse 1

||G | G7 |C |G
A - mazing Grace! How sweet the sound
|G | |D |D7
That saved a wretch like me!
|G |G7 |C |G
I once was lost, but now am found,
|G |D D7|G C/G|G
Was blind, but now I see.

Verse 2

||G | G7|C |G
'Twas grace that taught my heart to fear
|G | |D |D7
And grace my fears re - lieved.
|G |G7 |C |G
How precious did that grace ap - pear
|G |D D7|G C/G|G
The hour I first be - lieved.

Verse 3

```
        ‖G      |       G7 |C          |G
Through  many  dan - gers,  toils,  and  snares,
 |G      |       |D        |D7
I  have  al - ready  come.
    |G          |G7          |C          |G
'Tis  grace  hath  brought  me  safe  thus  far,
    |G          |D    D7 |G      C/G |G
And  grace  will  lead  me  home.
```

Verse 4

```
    ‖G          |       G7 |C          |G
The  Lord  has  prom - ised  good  to  me;
    |G      |       |D        |D7
His  word  my  hope  se - cures.
    |G      |G7      |C          |G
He  will  my  shield  and  portion  be
    |G      |D    D7 |G      C/G |G          ‖
As  long  as  life  en - dures.
```

At the Cross

Words by Isaac Watts and Ralph E. Hudson
Music by Ralph E. Hudson

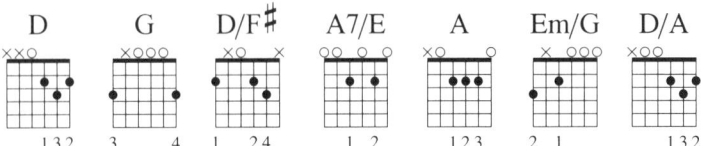

Verse 1

‖**D** |
A - las! and did my Savior bleed?
|**G** **D/F♯** **A7/E** **D** |**A**
And did my Sov - 'reign die?
D | |
Would He devote that sacred head
|**Em/G** **D/A** **A7**|**D**
For sinners such as I?

Refrain

‖**D** |**A7**
At the cross, at the cross where I first saw the light
|**A7** |**D**
And the burden of my heart rolled a - way,
|**G** |**D**
It was there by faith I re - ceived my sight,
|**Em/G** **A7** |**D**
And now I am happy all the day!

Verse 2

‖**D** |
Was it for crimes that I have done
|**G** **D/F♯** **A7/E** **D** |**A**
He groaned up - on the tree?
D | |
A - mazing pity! Grace unknown!
|**Em/G** **D/A** **A7** |**D**
And love be - yond de - gree!

Repeat Refrain

Verse 3

‖**D** |
Well, might the sun in darkness hole
    |**G**   **D/F♯ A7/E D** |**A**
And shut his glo‑ries in,
D | |
When Christ, the mighty Maker, died
    |**Em/G**   **D/A**   **A7** |**D**
For man, the crea‑ture's sin.

Repeat Refrain

Verse 4

‖**D** |
But drops of grief can ne'er repay
    |**G**   **D/F♯ A7/E** **D**|**A**
The debt of love I owe.
D | |
Here, Lord, I give my‑self away.
    |**Em/G**   **D/A A7** |**D**   ‖
'Tis all that I   can do!

Repeat Refrain

Be Thou My Vision

Traditional Irish
TRANSLATED by Mary E. Byrne

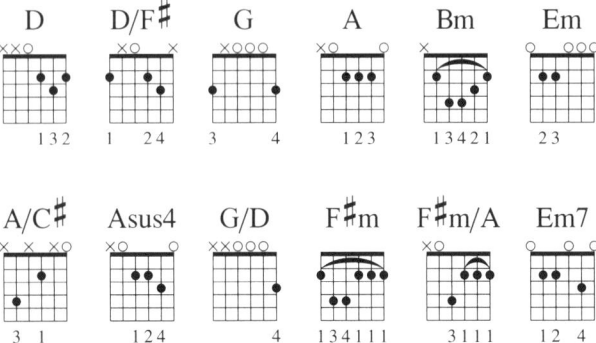

Verse 1

```
    D         D/F# G  A
Be Thou my  vi - sion,
G |D/F# Bm A |D          |
O Lord of my heart;
A         Em |A/C# D  D/F#|
Naught be all else to me,
G   D/F# Bm |Asus4     A  |
Save that Thou art.
G            |G/D   D
Thou my best thought,
   |A/C# Bm F#m|G        A  |
By day  or  by   night,
Bm      F#m/A |G      Bm
Waking or      sleep - ing,
D/F# |G       Em7 |D          ||
Thy  presence my  light.
```

Verse 2

```
       D        D/F#|G   A
Be Thou my  wis - dom,
G  |D/F# Bm A  |D              |
And Thou my true word;
A    Em|A/C#D
I  ev - er  with  Thee
D/F#|G     D/F# Bm |Asus4      A |
And Thou with  me, Lord.
G                 |G/D  D       |
Thou and Thou on  -  ly,
A/C# Bm F#m|G              A  |
First  in   my   heart,
Bm        F#m/A |G     Bm
Great God of      Heav - en,
D/F#|G        Em7 |D            ||
My   treasure Thou art.
```

Verse 3

```
       D         D/F# |G      A
Great God of    Heav - en,
G  |D/F# Bm  A |D             |
My vic - to - ry  won,
A    Em  |A/C#  D   D/F#|
May I reach Heav - en's joys,
G D/F#  Bm      |Asus4     A  |
O bright heav'n's Sun!
G            |G/D  D
Heart of my own heart,
     |A/C# Bm F#m|G          A |
What - ev - er  be - fall,
Bm      F#m/A |G    Bm
Still be my    vi - sion,
D/F#|G      Em7|D             ||
O    Ruler of  all.
```

Bringing in the Sheaves

Words by Knowles Shaw
Music by George A. Minor

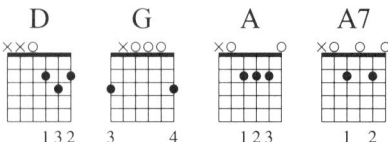

Verse 1

D | G |
Sowing in the morning, sowing seeds of kindness,
D |A |
Sowing in the noontide and the dewy eve;
D | G |
Waiting for the harvest, and the time of reaping,
D |A7 D ||
We shall come rejoicing, bringing in the sheaves.

Refrain

D |G D |
Bringing in the sheaves,   bringing in the sheaves,
D | A7 |
We shall come rejoicing, bringing in the sheaves;
D |G D |
Bringing in the sheaves,   bringing in the sheaves,
D |A7 D ||
We shall come rejoicing, bringing in the sheaves.

Verse 2

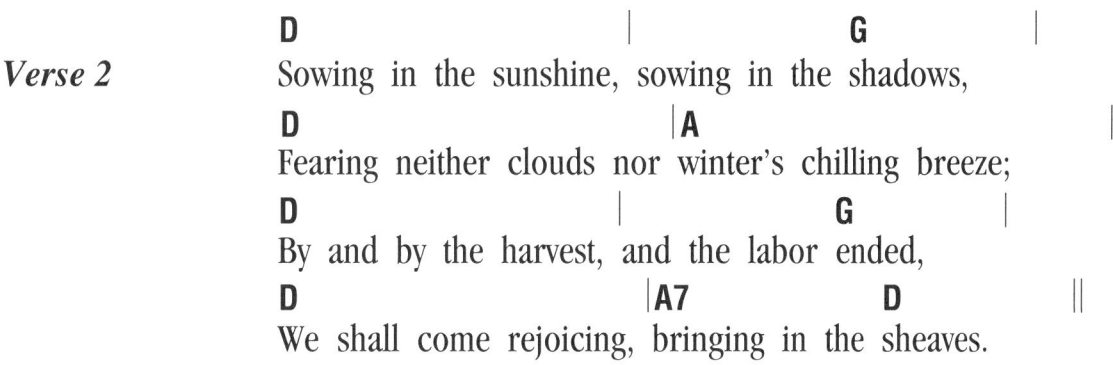

```
D                          |              G          |
Sowing in the sunshine, sowing in the shadows,
D                          |A                        |
Fearing neither clouds nor winter's chilling breeze;
D                          |              G          |
By and by the harvest, and the labor ended,
D                          |A7            D         ||
We shall come rejoicing, bringing in the sheaves.
```

Repeat Refrain

Verse 3

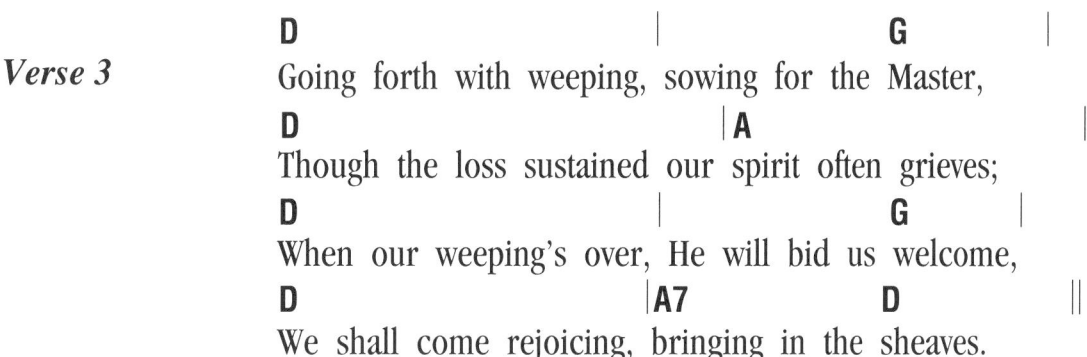

```
D                          |              G          |
Going forth with weeping, sowing for the Master,
D                          |A                        |
Though the loss sustained our spirit often grieves;
D                          |              G          |
When our weeping's over, He will bid us welcome,
D                          |A7            D         ||
We shall come rejoicing, bringing in the sheaves.
```

Repeat Refrain

Christ the Lord Is Risen Today

Words by Charles Wesley
Music by Robert Williams

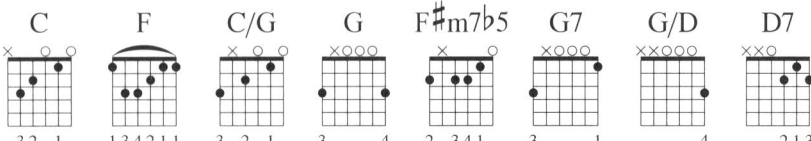

Verse 1

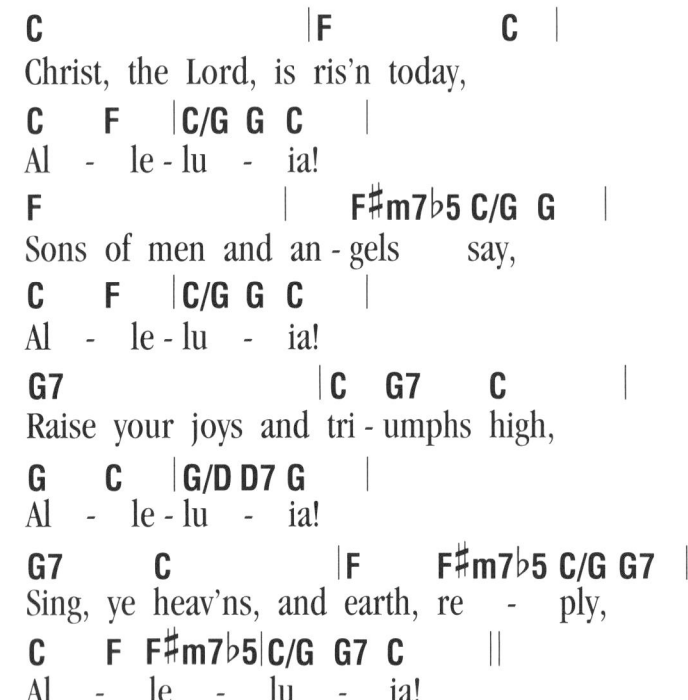

```
   C                   |F        C   |
Christ, the Lord, is ris'n today,
   C   F   |C/G G  C    |
Al - le - lu - ia!
   F                 |    F#m7♭5 C/G  G    |
Sons of men and an - gels     say,
   C   F   |C/G G  C    |
Al - le - lu - ia!
   G7                |C   G7    C      |
Raise your joys and tri - umphs high,
   G    C   |G/D D7  G    |
Al - le - lu - ia!
   G7     C           |F    F#m7♭5 C/G  G7  |
Sing, ye heav'ns, and earth, re - ply,
   C   F  F#m7♭5|C/G G7 C      ||
Al - le - lu - ia!
```

Verse 2

```
C                    |F              C  |
Lives again our glorious King,
C    F   |C/G G  C       |
Al  - le - lu  -  ia!
F                |       F♯m7♭5 C/G   G   |
Where, O death, is now thy      sting?
C    F   |C/G G  C       |
Al  - le - lu  -  ia!
G7               |C   G7  C          |
Dying  once, He all doth save,
G    C   |G/D D7  G      |
Al  - le - lu  -  ia!
G7        C      |F  F♯m7♭5 C/G   G7 |
Where thy victory, O          grave?
C    F  F♯m7♭5|C/G  G7 C       ||
Al  - le  -  lu  -  ia!
```

Verse 3

```
C                    |F              C  |
Love's redeeming work is done,
C    F   |C/G G  C       |
Al  - le - lu  -  ia!
F                |       F♯m7♭5 C/G  G  |
Fought the fight, the bat - tle     won,
C    F   |C/G G  C       |
Al  - le - lu  -  ia!
G7                 |C   G7  C          |
Death in vain for - bids Him rise,
G    C   |G/D D7  G      |
Al  - le - lu  -  ia!
G7        C      |F   F♯m7♭5 C/G   G7 |
Christ has opened Par - a  -   dise,
C    F  F♯m7♭5|C/G  G7 C       ||
Al  - le  -  lu  -  ia!
```

17

Come, Thou Fount of Every Blessing

Words by Robert Robinson
Music from John Wyeth's Repository of Sacred Music

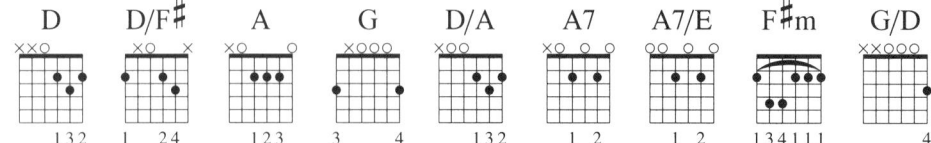

Verse 1

‖D   D/F♯|A
Come, Thou Fount of ev - 'ry blessing,

D D/F♯|G D D/A A7 |D
Tune my heart to sing Thy grace.

    A7|D   D/F♯|A
Streams of mercy, nev - er ceasing,

D D/F♯|G D D/A A7 |D
Call for songs of loud - est praise.

D/F♯ A7/E|D F♯mG D |G/D D
Teach me some me - lo - dious son - net,

D/F♯ A7/E|D F♯m G   D|
Sung by flam - ing tongues a - bove.

   A7 |D   D/F♯|A
Praise His name; I'm fixed up - on it,

D D/F♯ |G D D/A A7 |D
Name of God's re - deem - ing love.

Verse 2

```
          A7 ‖D              D/F♯ |A
Hith - er - to Thy love has   blest me;
D      D/F♯ |G        D   D/A A7 |D
Thou has   brought me to  this place.
          A7|D                D/F♯ |A
And I   know Thy hand will   bring me
D      D/F♯|G      D   D/A A7      |D
Safe - ly    home by Thy good grace.
D/F♯ A7/E |D      F♯m G       D|G/D   D
Je - sus  sought me   when a stran - ger,
D/F♯  A7/E |D      F♯m G     D |
Wan - d'ring from the   fold of God.
          A7|D             D/F♯ |A
He, to rescue me from danger,
D         D/F♯|G      D   D/A A7    |D
Bought me   with His pre - cious blood.
```

Verse 3

```
          A7‖D                  D/F♯|A
O, to grace how great a     debtor
D    D/F♯|G  D    D/A      A7|D
Dai - ly    I'm con - strained to be!
          A7 |D              D/F♯|A
Let Thy goodness like a     fetter,
D    D/F♯|G    D    D/A   A7|D
Bind my   wan - d'ring heart to Thee.
D/F♯   A7/E|D     F♯m G       D|G/D D
Prone to    wan - der, Lord, I feel it,
D/F♯   A7/E|D     F♯m G    D|
Prone to    leave the   God I love.
          A7 |D                D/F♯|A
Here's my heart, O, take and   seal it;
D   D/F♯|G  D   D/A   A7|D              ‖
Seal it    for Thy courts a - bove.
```

Faith of Our Fathers

Words by Frederick William Faber
Music by Henri F. Hemy and James G. Walton

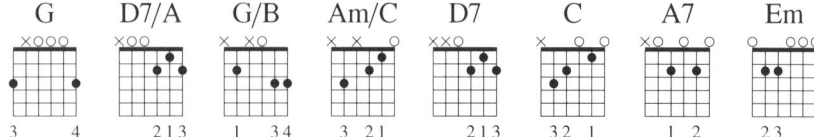

G   D7/A   G/B   Am/C   D7   C   A7   Em

Verse 1

```
G                |      D7/A G/B |Am/C D7 |G            |
Faith of our fa  -   thers,  liv - ing still,
C           |G        |A7        |D            |
In  spite of dungeon, fire,   and sword;
G                |      D7/A G/B |Am/C D7 |G            |
O  how our hearts     beat high   with joy
C           |G        |A7     D7 |G            ||
Whene'er we hear that glo - rious word!
```

Refrain

```
C         |G     |D    |G         |
Faith of our fathers,  holy    faith!
G         |C     Em|D    D7 |G         ||
We will be true  to   thee   till death.
```

Verse 2

```
G              |  D7/A G/B  |Am/C D7 |G           |
Faith of our fa  -  thers, we    will strive
C          |G      |A7     |D          |
To win all nations unto     thee;
G              |      D7/A G/B |Am/C    D7 |G           |
And through the truth      that comes    from God,
C              |G      |A7    D7|G          ||
Mankind shall then be tru - ly free.
```

Repeat Refrain

Verse 3

```
G              |  D7/A G/B  |Am/C D7 |G           |
Faith of our fa  -  thers, we    will love
C          |G      |A7     |D          |
Both friend and foe   in all   our strife;
G              |  D7/A G/B|Am/C D7    |G           |
And preach thee, too,     all love   knows how,
C          |G          |A7    D7 |G          ||
By kindly words and vir - tuous life.
```

Repeat Refrain

For the Beauty of the Earth

Words by Folliot S. Pierpoint
Music by Conrad Kocher

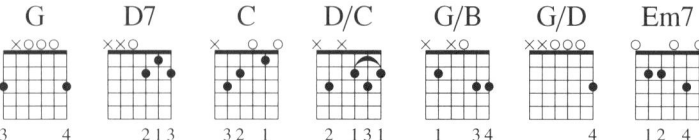

Verse 1

G   D7   G |C   D7   G |
For the beau - ty of the earth,

C   D/C G/B C |G/D D7 G |
For the glo - ry of   the skies,

G   D7 G |C   D7 G |
For the love which from our birth

C D/C G/B C |G/D   D7 G ||
O - ver   and a - round us lies.

Refrain

G   D7 Em7 G |D7   G |
Lord of all,   to Thee we raise

C   D7 G   C |G/D   D7 G ||
This, our hymn of grate - ful praise.

Verse 2

```
G        D7   G│C  D7   G              │
For the beau-ty of each hour
C  D/C G/B C  │G/D D7  G               │
Of the day and of  the night,
G        D7   G │C   D7  G             │
Hill and vale, and tree and flower,
C  D/C G/B   C  │G/D D7 G            ‖
Sun and moon, and stars of light.
```

Repeat Refrain

Verse 3

```
G       D7 G │C   D7  G            │
For the joy of ear and eye,
C   D/C G/B   C  │G/D   D7  G             │
For the heart and mind's de-light,
G        D7   G │C    D7   G          │
For the mys-tic har-mo-ny
C    D/C G/B   C │G/D   D7  G            ‖
Link-ing sense to sound and sight.
```

Repeat Refrain

Verse 4

```
G       D7 G │C    D7   G           │
For the joy of hu-man love,
C    D/C G/B C  │G/D D7  G               │
Bro-ther, sis-ter, par-ent, child,
G            D7   G │C      D7 G          │
Friends on earth and friends a-bove,
C  D/C G/B C │G/D    D7  G            ‖
For all gen-tle thoughts and mild.
```

Repeat Refrain

God of Grace and God of Glory

Words by Harry Emerson Fosdick
Music by John Hughes

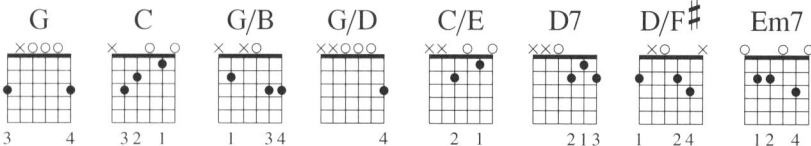

Verse 1

```
 G    C  G/B      |G     C G/D  D  |
God of grace and God of  glo - ry,
 G   C/E C     |G/D  D7  G      |
On Thy people pour Thy power.
 G    C    G/B  |G     C G/D  D  |
Crown Thine ancient church's  sto - ry;
 G    C   G/B  C |G/D  D7   G      |
Bring her bud to glo - rious flower.
 D7   G/D  D7    |G    D7  G      |
Grant us  wisdom, grant us courage,
 G       D7  G   D/F# Em7 |D7            |
For the fac - ing of  this   hour,
 G/B  D7  G   C |G/D  D7  G        ||
For the fac - ing of  this hour.
```

Verse 2

```
G    C  G/B    |G  C G/D    D   |
```
Lo! the hosts of evil 'round us;
```
G     C/E  C       |G/D D7  G         |
```
Scorn Thy Christ, as - sail His ways!
```
G     C   G/B     |G        C G/D    D   |
```
Fears and doubts too long have   bound us;
```
G    C   G/B   C |G/D  D7 G           |
```
Free our hearts to work and praise.
```
D7    G/D D7      |G     D7 G          |
```
Grant us   wisdom, grant us courage,
```
G         D7 G   D/F♯ Em7 |D7              |
```
For the liv - ing of   these days,
```
G/B D7 G    C |G/D D7    G        ||
```
For the liv - ing of   these days.

Verse 3

```
G    C  G/B     |G      C G/D   D   |
```
Cure Thy children's warring   mad - ness;
```
G    C/E C      |G/D D7   G         |
```
Bend our pride to Thy con - trol.
```
G     C  G/B  |G       C G/D   D    |
```
Shame our wanton self - ish   glad - ness,
```
G   C G/B   C |G/D  D7 G          |
```
Rich in things and poor in soul.
```
D7   G/D D7      |G     D7 G         |
```
Grant us   wisdom, grant us courage,
```
G      D7   G   D/F♯ Em7 |D7            |
```
Lest we miss Thy king - dom's goal,
```
G/B D7 G    C |G/D  D7    G       ||
```
Lest we miss Thy king - dom's goal.

God of Our Fathers

Words by Daniel Crane Roberts
Music by George William Warren

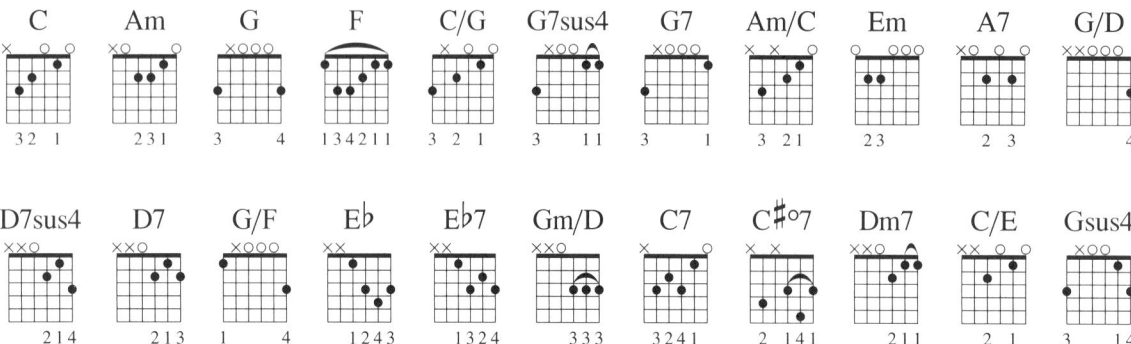

Verse 1

C Am G |C   F |
God of   our fa - thers,

C/G   G7sus4 G7 |C |
Whose al - might - y hand

C Am/C |Em   A7 |
Leads forth in beau - ty,

G/D   D7sus4 D7 |G |
All the star - ry band

G G/F |E♭ |
Of shining worlds

E♭7 |Gm/D   D7sus4 D7 |G   G7 |
In splendor through the skies,

**C   F |C   C7 **
Our grateful songs

C♯○7 |Dm7 C/E Gsus4 G7 |C ||
Be - fore Thy throne a - rise.

Verse 2

C   Am G |C
Thy love di - vine

F |C/G   G7sus4 G7 |C |
Hath led us in   the past.

C Am/C |Em
In this free land

A7|G/D   D7sus4 D7 |G |
By Thee our lot   is cast.

G G/F |E♭   E♭7 |
Be Thou our rul - er,

Gm/D   D7sus4 D7 |G   G7 |
Guardian, guide, and stay,

C F |C   C7
Thy word our law,

C♯○7|Dm7 C/E Gsus4 G7 |C ||
Thy paths our cho - sen way.

Verse 3

C Am G |C   F |
Re - fresh Thy peo - ple

C/G   G7sus4 G7 |C |
On their toil - some way.

C   Am/C |Em
Lead us from night

A7|G/D D7sus4 D7 |G |
To never-end - ing day.

G G/F |E♭
Fill all our lives

E♭7 |Gm/D   D7sus4 D7|G   G7 |
With love and grace di - vine,

C F |C   C7
And glory, laud,

C♯○7 |Dm7 C/E Gsus4 G7|C ||
And praise be ev - er Thine!

Holy, Holy, Holy! Lord God Almighty

Words by Reginald Heber
Music by John B. Dykes

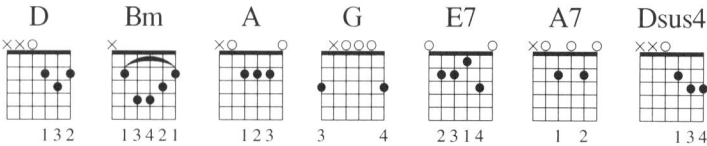

Verse 1

|D Bm |A D |
Holy, holy, ho - ly!

|G |D |
Lord God Al - migh - ty!

|A D A |Bm E7 A
Early in the morn - ing

|D |A E7 |A A7 |
Our song shall rise to Thee.

|D Bm |A D |
Holy, holy, ho - ly!

|G |D |
Merciful and mighty!

|Bm D |G D |
God in three Per - sons,

|G A7 |Dsus4 D ||
Blessed Trini - ty!

Verse 2

```
      D     Bm |A    D      |
Holy, holy, ho - ly!
      G              |D          |
All the saints a - dore Thee,
      A      D     A |Bm   E7  A
Casting down their gold - en crowns
      D |A        E7    |A          A7  |
A - round the glassy sea.
      D     Bm   |A    D        |
Cheru - bim and sera - phim
      G              |D              |
Falling down be - fore Thee,
      Bm    D       |G
Which wert, and art,
      D  |G    A7         |Dsus4  D     ||
And ever - more shall be.
```

Verse 3

```
      D     Bm |A    D      |
Holy, holy, ho - ly!
      G                 |D          |
Though the darkness hide Thee,
      A           D    A |Bm  E7  A
Though the eye of sin - ful man
      D  |A   E7       |A          A7  |
Thy glory may not see.
      D    Bm      |A    D      |
Only Thou art ho - ly;
      G                |D              |
There is none be - side Thee,
      Bm  D      |G     D
Per - fect in pow - er,
      D |G       A7  |Dsus4  D      ||
In love and puri - ty.
```

How Can I Keep from Singing

Words and Music by Rev. Robert Lowrey (1869)

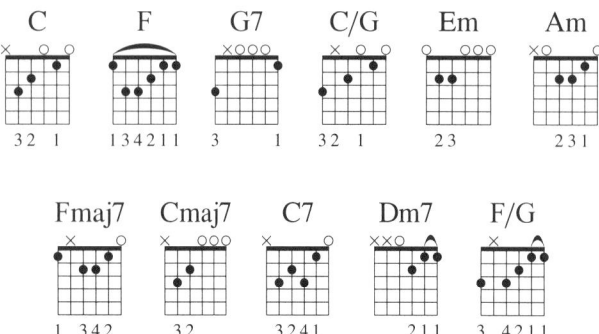

Verse 1

|C|F|
My life flows on in endless song

|C|G7|
A - bove earth's lamen - tation.

|C|F|
I hear the real, though far-off hymn

|C/G|G7|C|
That hails a new cre - ation.

|Em|Am|
No storm can shake my inmost calm

|Fmaj7|C/G|G7|
While to that rock I'm clinging.

|C|Cmaj7|C7|F|Dm7|
It sounds an ech - o in my soul.

|C/G|G7|C|F/G|
How can I keep from singing?

Verse 2

```
        ‖C                    |F
What though the tempest 'round me rears,
  |C                  |G7
I know the truth; it liveth.
      |C                    |F
What though the darkness 'round me close,
     |C/G         G7|C
Songs in the night, it  giveth.
       |Em                   |Am
No storm can shake my inmost calm
      |Fmaj7           |C/G           G7
While to that rock I'm clinging.
         |C     Cmaj7  C7  |F          Dm7
Since love is lord        of Heav'n and earth,
       |C/G          G7 |C              F/G
How can I keep from singing?
```

Verse 3

```
        ‖C                  |F
When tyrants tremble, sick with fear,
   |C                        |G7
And hear their death knells ringing,
     |C                  |F
When friends rejoice both far and near,
     |C/G           G7  |C
How can I keep from singing?
     |Em                 |Am
In prison cell and dungeon vile,
      |Fmaj7              |C/G          G7
Our thoughts to them are winging.
        |C        Cmaj7     C7  |F      Dm7
When friends by shame       are unde - filed,
       |C/G          G7 |C                ‖
How can I keep from singing?
```

I Love to Tell the Story

Words by A. Catherine Hankey
Music by William G. Fischer

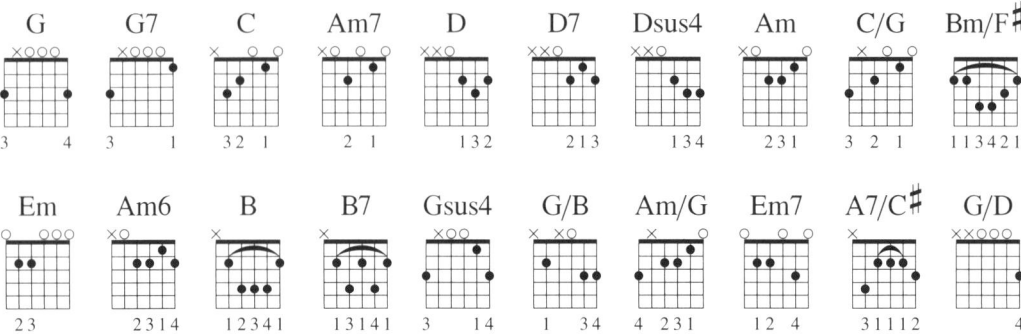

Verse 1

||G | G7|C   Am7 |G
I love to tell the story of unseen things a - bove,

|D   G |D7 G | C |Dsus4 D
Of Jesus and His glo - ry, of Jesus and His love.

|D7   Am|C/G G Bm/F♯ |Em   Am6|B
I love to tell the sto - ry be - cause I know it's true;

B7|C   Am7|C/G G |D7 |Gsus4 G Am7
It satisfies my long - ings as nothing else can do.

Refrain

G/B||D |Am/G G |C   D7|C/G G
I love to tell the sto - ry! 'Twill be my theme in glo - ry

Bm/F♯|Em7 G |C A7/C♯ |G/D D7 |Gsus4   G
To tell the old, old story of Jesus and His love.

Verse 2

```
          ||G                    |         G7  |C          Am7 |G
          I love to tell the story, more wonder-ful, it seems,
              |D            G |D7 G     |            C  |Dsus4  D
          Than all the gol-den fan-cies of all our gol-den dreams.
              |D7           Am|C/G  G  Bm/F♯|Em          Am6|B
          I love to tell the sto-ry; it      did so much for  me,
          B7 |C              Am7|C/G  G    |D7            |Gsus4  G  Am7
          And that is just the  rea-son I tell it now to thee.
```

Repeat Refrain

Verse 3

```
          ||G                    |         G7|C          Am7 |G
          I love to tell the story; 'tis pleasant to re-peat
              |D                G|D7 G     |            C |Dsus4  D
          What seems, each time I tell it, more wonderful-ly sweet.
              |D7           Am|C/G  G  Bm/F♯|Em          Am6 |B
          I love to tell the sto-ry, for     some have nev-er    heard
          B7 |C              Am7|C/G  G    |D7            |Gsus4  G  Am7
          The message of sal-va-tion from God's own holy word.
```

Repeat Refrain

Immortal, Invisible

Words by Walter Chalmers Smith
Traditional Welsh Melody
From John Roberts' Canaidau y Cyssegr

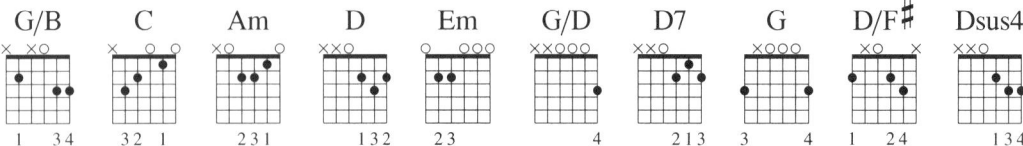

G/B   C   Am   D   Em   G/D   D7   G   D/F#   Dsus4

Verse 1

```
    ‖C        Am|D      Em |G/D        D7|G
    Im - mortal, in - visi - ble, God on - ly  wise,
    G/B|C        Am |D      Em |G/D        D7 |G
    In  light in - ac - cessi - ble hid from  our  eyes,
         |Em        D/F#|G  G/B  Em |G/B          |Dsus4 D
    Most blessed, most glo - rious, the Ancient of Days,
    G |C        Am |D      Em |G/D        D7 |G
    Al - mighty, vic - torious, Thy great Name we praise.
```

Verse 2

```
    ‖C        Am |D        Em |G/D  D7|G
    Un - resting, un - hasting, and silent as light,
    G/B|C        Am |D        Em |G/D  D7|G
    Nor wanting, nor wasting, Thou rulest in might.
         |Em        D/F#|G        G/B  Em |G/B          |Dsus4 D
    Thy justice, like moun - tains, high soaring a - bove
    G |C        Am|D        Em|G/D        D7 |G
    Thy clouds, which are fountains of goodness and love.
```

Verse 3

```
      ‖C        Am  |D      Em|G/D        D7  |G
```
To all, life Thou givest, to both great and small;
```
G/B |C        Am  |D      Em |G/D      D7|G
```
In all life Thou livest, the true life of all.
```
       |Em        D/F♯|G      G/B Em|G/B            |Dsus4  D
```
We blossom and flour - ish as leaves on the tree,
```
G  |C        Am |D      Em |G/D              D7 |G
```
And wither and perish but naught chang - eth Thee.

Verse 4

```
        ‖C        Am|D      Em  |G/D        D7|G
```
Thou reignest in glory, Thou dwellest in light;
```
G/B  |C        Am |D              Em|G/D    D7  |G
```
Thine angels a - dore Thee, all veiling their sight.
```
       |Em        D/F♯  |G      G/B Em |G/B            |Dsus4  D
```
All laud we would ren - der; O help us to see
```
G  |C        Am |D        Em|G/D        D7 |G              ‖
```
'Tis only the splendor of light hid - eth Thee.

Jerusalem

By C. H. Parry

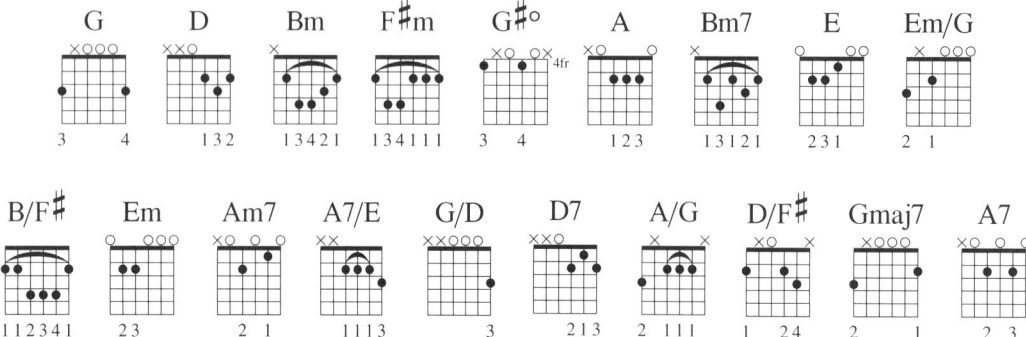

Verse 1

```
                 ‖G              |D
And  did  those  feet  in  ancient  times
G          |D          Bm          |G
Walk  upon  England's  mountains  green?
          D        |Bm  F♯m      |Bm  G♯°
And  was  the  Holy  Lamb  of  God
       A        |Bm7      F♯m  E  |A
On  England's  pleasant  past - ures  seen?
       Em/G  B/F♯ |Em        A7        |Em
And  did    the   counte - nance  di - vine
        A7/E      |G/D      D7        |G
Shine  forth  up - on  our  clouded  hills?
               |Em      A    A/G  |D/F♯
And  was  Je - rusa - lem  builded  here
       G        |D/F♯    Gmaj7  A7 |D                    |
A - mong  these  dark  sa - ta  -  nic  mills?
```

Verse 2

```
          ‖G                    |D
Bring me my bow of burning gold!
G              |D      Bm     |G
Bring me my arrows of de - sire!
        D      |Bm      F♯m          |Bm G♯°
Bring me my spear! O clouds, un - fold!
        A       |Bm7   F♯m E |A
Bring me my chari - ot    of fire!
   Em/G B/F♯ |Em              Am7    |Em
I will   not   cease from mental fight,
      A7/E      |G/D             D7      |G
Nor shall my sword sleep in my hand
              |Em   A      A/G  |D/F♯
Till we have built  Je - rusa - lem
    G         |D/F♯        Gmaj7 A7 |D                    ‖
In England's green and pleas - ant land.
```

Jesus Christ Is Risen Today

Words and Music from Lyra Davidica

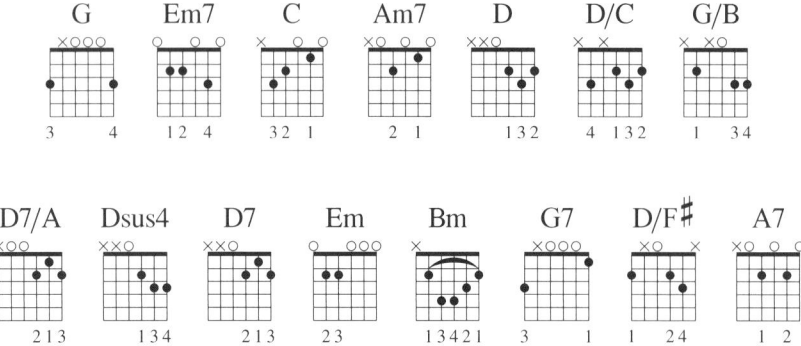

Verse 1

G   Em7 |C   Am7 D   D/C |
Jesus Christ is risen to - day,

G/B D7/A G   C |Dsus4 D G |
Al -   le - lu - ia!

G   Em7 |C   Am7 D   D/C |
Our tri - umphant ho - ly   day,

G/B D7/A G   C |Dsus4 D G |
Al -   le - lu - ia!

Em Bm G7 |C Am7 Dsus4 D |
Who did once, up - on the   cross,

G   D/F# Em7 A7|Dsus4   D7 |
Al -   le - lu - ia!

G   Em7 |C   Am7 D   D/C |
Suffer to re - deem our loss.

G/B D7/A G   C |Dsus4 D G ||
Al -   le - lu - ia!

Verse 2

```
G        Em7        |C  Am7 D    D/C      |
Hymns of praise then let us    sing,
G/B D7/A  G    C  |Dsus4  D  G            |
Al    -    le - lu    -    ia!
G     Em7        |C        Am7 D    D/C   |
Unto Christ, our heav'n - ly    King,
G/B D7/A  G    C  |Dsus4  D  G            |
Al    -    le - lu    -    ia!
Em  Bm  G7        |C     Am7 Dsus4  D     |
Who en - dured the cross and   grave,
G   D/F♯ Em7 A7 |Dsus4        D7          |
Al    -    le - lu    -    ia!
G        Em7 |C     Am7 D    D/C          |
Sinners to re - deem and   save.
G/B D7/A  G    C  |Dsus4  D  G            ‖
Al    -    le - lu    -    ia!
```

Verse 3

```
G        Em7        |C  Am7 D     D/C     |
But the pains which He en  -  dured,
G/B D7/A  G    C  |Dsus4  D  G            |
Al    -    le - lu    -    ia!
G        Em7 |C     Am7 D     D/C         |
Our sal - vation have  pro - cured.
G/B D7/A  G    C  |Dsus4  D  G            |
Al    -    le - lu    -    ia!
Em  Bm  G7        |C  Am7 Dsus4  D        |
Now a  -  bove the sky He's king,
G   D/F♯ Em7 A7 |Dsus4        D7          |
Al    -    le - lu    -    ia!
G        Em7 |C  Am7 D    D/C             |
Where the angels ev - er    sing.
G/B D7/A  G    C  |Dsus4  D  G            ‖
Al    -    le - lu    -    ia!
```

Joyful, Joyful, We Adore Thee

Words by Henry van Dyke
Music by Ludwig van Beethoven, melody from Ninth Symphony
Adapted by Edward Hodges

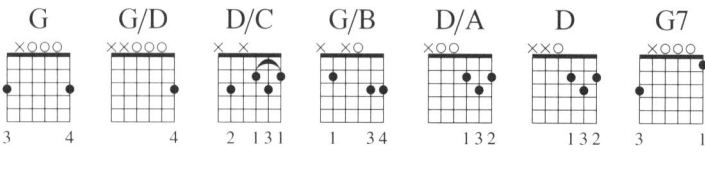

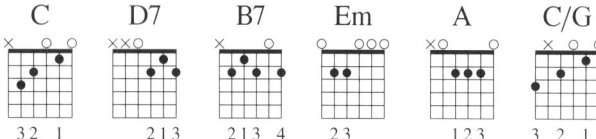

Verse 1

G   **|G/D**   **D/C**   **|**
Joyful, joyful, we adore Thee,

G/B   **D/A** **G** **|G/D** **D**   **|**
God of glo - ry, Lord of love.

G   **G7** **|C**   **|**
Hearts unfold like flow'rs before Thee,

G/D   **|D7**   **G**   **|**
Op'ning to the sun a - bove.

D   **G/D**   **|D**   **G/D**   **|**
Melt the clouds of sin and sadness;

D   **B7**   **|Em**   **A**   **D**   **|**
Drive the dark of doubt a - way.

G   **C/G** **G7** **|C**   **|**
Giver of im - mortal gladness,

G/D   **|D7**   **G**   **||**
Fill us with the light of day!

Verse 2

```
G                    |G/D          D/C |
All Thy works with joy surround Thee;
G/B      D/A   G |G/D  D            |
Earth and heav'n re - flect Thy rays.
G              G7 |C                |
Stars and an - gels sing around Thee,
G/D             |D7     G        |
Center of un - broken praise.
D        G/D  |D         G/D      |
Field and forest, vale and mountain,
D      B7     |Em    A    D       |
Flow'ry meadow, flash - ing sea,
G        C/G  G7 |C               |
Chanting bird and flowing fountain
G/D             |D7      G        ||
Call us to re - joice in Thee.
```

Verse 3

```
G                |G/D          D/C |
Thou art giving and forgiv - ing,
G/B D/A   G  |G/D  D           |
Ever bless - ing, ev - er blest,
G              G7 |C            |
Wellspring of the joy of living,
G/D             |D7     G       |
Ocean depth of happy rest!
D        G/D  |D          G/D    |
Thou our Father, Christ our Brother,
D      B7     |Em   A    D       |
All who live in love are Thine.
G        C/G  G7|C               |
Teach us how to love each other;
G/D             |D7     G       ||
Lift us to the joy di - vine.
```

Just a Closer Walk with Thee

Traditional

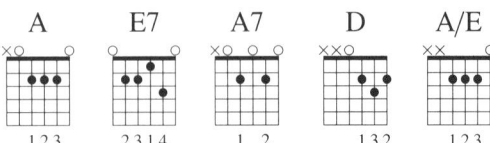

Verse 1

A |**E7** |
I am weak, but Thou art strong;

E7 |**A** |
Jesus, keep me from all wrong.

A   **A7** |**D**
I'll be satisfied as long

     |**A/E**   **E7** |**A**   ‖
As I walk, dear Lord, close to Thee.

Refrain

A |**E7** |
Just a closer walk with Thee;

E7 |**A** |
Grant it, Jesus, is my plea,

A   **A7** |**D**
Daily walking close to Thee,

     |**A/E**   **E7** |**A**   ‖
Let it be, dear Lord, let it be.

Verse 2

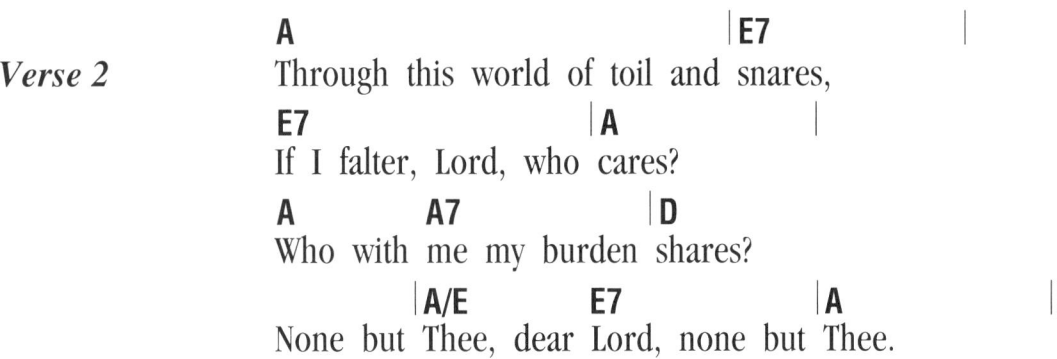

```
A                              |E7                  |
Through this world of toil and snares,
E7                   |A              |
If I falter, Lord, who cares?
A        A7           |D
Who with me my burden shares?
        |A/E        E7            |A            ||
None but Thee, dear Lord, none but Thee.
```

Repeat Refrain

Verse 3

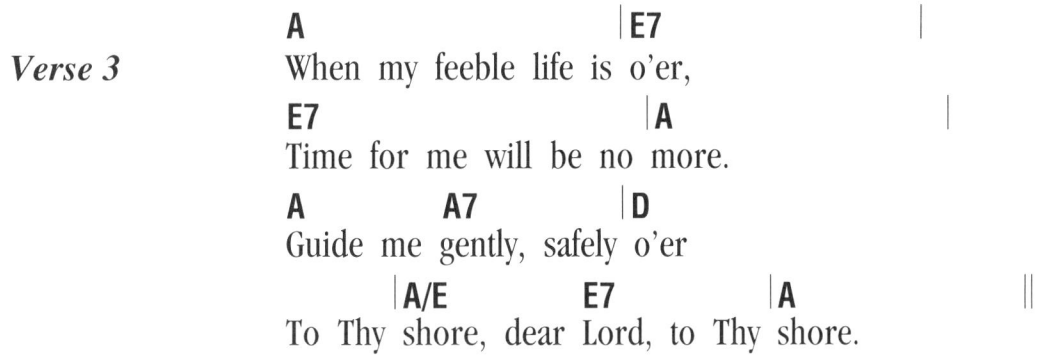

```
A                         |E7                 |
When my feeble life is o'er,
E7                       |A              |
Time for me will be no more.
A        A7           |D
Guide me gently, safely o'er
        |A/E        E7          |A            ||
To Thy shore, dear Lord, to Thy shore.
```

Repeat Refrain

The King of Love My Shepherd Is

Words by Henry Baker
Traditional Irish Melody

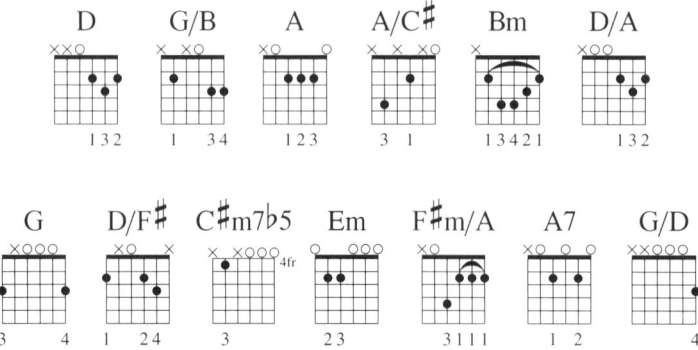

Verse 1

‖D   G/B│A   A/C♯│D   A   │Bm
The King of love my shep - herd is,
│D/A   G   │D/F♯ G │D   │
Whose good - ness fail - eth nev - er.
│Bm   C♯m7♭5│D   Em│D/F♯ A   │Bm
I noth - ing   lack if I   am His
F♯m/A│D/F♯ G │D/A A7 │D   G/D│D
And   He   is mine for - ev   -   er.

Verse 2

‖D   G/B│A   A/C♯│D   A │Bm
Where streams of liv - ing wa - ter flow,
│D/A   G   │D/F♯ G │D   │
My ran - somed soul He lead - eth.
│Bm   C♯m7♭5│D   Em │D/F♯ A   │Bm
And where the   ver - dant pas - tures grow,
F♯m/A│D/F♯ G   │D/A A7 │D   G/D│D
With   food ce - les - tial feed - eth.

Verse 3

‖D　　　G/B ‖A　　　A/C♯‖D　A‖Bm
Per - verse and fool - ish　oft I strayed,
　　　‖D/A　G ‖D/F♯ G ‖D　　　‖
But yet in love He sought me,
　　　‖Bm C♯m7♭5‖D　　　Em ‖D/F♯　A ‖Bm
And on His　　shoul - der gen - tly laid,
F♯m/A‖D/F♯　G ‖D/A　A7 ‖D　　　G/D‖D
And　　home, re - joic - ing, brought　　me.

Verse 4

‖D　　　G/B ‖A　　A/C♯‖D　　A ‖Bm
In death's dark vale I　　fear no ill
　　　‖D/A　　G　‖D/F♯ G ‖D　　　‖
With Thee, dear Lord, be - side　　me.
　　　‖Bm　C♯m7♭5‖D　　Em‖D/F♯　　A ‖Bm
Thy rod and　　staff, my com - fort still;
F♯m/A ‖D/F♯　G ‖D/A　A7‖D　　G/D‖D　　　　　‖
Thy　　cross be - fore to guide　　me.

The King Shall Come

Text by John Brownlie
Music by William Croft

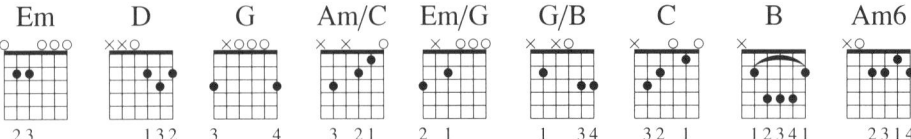

Verse 1

||Em   D   G   Am/C|D   Em/G Em
The King shall come when morn - ing dawns

G/B|C   D   G   Am/C|B
And light tri - um - phant breaks,

Em |G   C D   G/B|Am6 Em G
When beau - ty gilds the east - ern hills

G/B|C   D Em B|Em
And life to joy a - wakes.

Verse 2

||Em D G   Am/C|D Em/G Em
Not as of old a   lit - tle   child

G/B|C   D   G   Am/C|B
To bear and fight and die,

Em|G   C   D   G/B|Am6 Em G
But crowned with glo - ry like   the sun

G/B |C   D Em   B |Em
That lights the morn - ing sky.

Verse 3

‖Em   D G   Am/C‖D   Em/G Em
O bright - er than the   ris - ing   morn

G/B ‖C   D   G   Am/C‖B
When he, vic - tor - ious, rose,

Em ‖G   C   D   G/B ‖Am6 Em G
And left the lone - some place of   death,

G/B ‖C   D   Em   B ‖Em
Des - pite the rage of foes.

Verse 4

‖Em   D G   Am/C‖D   Em/G Em
O bright - er than that   glo - rious morn

G/B ‖C   D   G   Am/C‖B
Shall this fair morn - ing   be

Em ‖G   C   D   G/B‖Am6 Em G
When Christ, our King, in   beau - ty   comes

G/B‖C   D   Em B   ‖Em   ‖
And we his face shall see!

Kumbaya

Congo Folksong

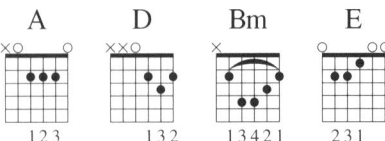

Verse 1

‖A | D |A |
Kumba - yah, my Lord,   Kumba - yah.

|A | Bm |E |
Kumba - yah, my Lord,   Kumba - yah.

|A | D |A |
Kumba - yah, my Lord,   Kumba - yah.

Bm |A E |A |
Oh   Lord, Kumba - yah.

Verse 2

‖A | D |A |
Someone's crying, Lord,   Kumba - yah.

|A | Bm |E |
Someone's crying, Lord,   Kumba - yah.

|A | D |A |
Someone's crying, Lord,   Kumba - yah.

Bm |A E |A |
Oh   Lord, Kumba - yah.

Verse 3

```
            ‖A              |   D      |A         |
     Someone's  singing,  Lord,     Kumba - yah.

             |A             |   Bm    |E         |
     Someone's  singing,  Lord,     Kumba - yah.

             |A             |   D      |A         |
     Someone's  singing,  Lord,     Kumba - yah.

     Bm     |A     E    |A        |          ‖
     Oh       Lord,  Kumba - yah.
```

Love Divine, All Loves Excelling

Words by Charles Wesley
Music by John Zundel

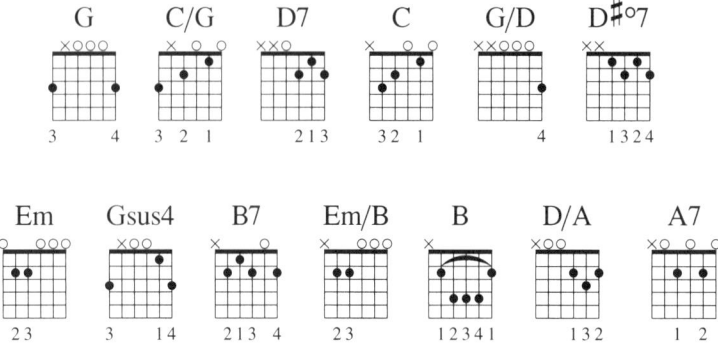

Verse 1

G   C/G G |D7   G |
Love di - vine, all loves ex - celling,

C |G/D D7   G |
Joy of heav'n to earth come down.

G   C/G G | D7 D#°7 Em |
Fix in us thy hum - ble dwell - ing,

C   G/D |D7   Gsus4 G |
All thy faithful mercies crown.

Em   B7 |Em/B   B |
Je - sus, Thou art all com - passion,

G   C/G   G |D/A A7   D   D7 |
Pure un - bound - ed love Thou art.

G C/G G | D7 D#°7 Em |
Visit us with Thy sal - va - tion;

C   G/D |D7   G ||
Enter ev'ry trembling heart.

Verse 2

G   C/G   G |D7   G |
Breathe, O breathe Thy loving Spirit.

C |G/D D7   G |
Into ev'ry trou - bled breast.

G   C/G G | D7 D♯°7 Em |
Let us all in Thee in - her - it,

C   G/D |D7   Gsus4 G |
Let us find that promised rest.

Em   B7 |Em/B   B |
Take away our bent to sinning,

G   C/G G |D/A A7 D   D7 |
Alpha and O - me - ga be.

G   C/G G | D7 D♯°7 Em |
End of faith, as its be - gin - ning,

C   G/D |D7   G ||
Set our hearts at liber - ty.

Verse 3

G   C/G   G |D7   G |
Come, Al - might - y, to de - liver;

C |G/D D7 G |
Let us all Thy life re - ceive.

G   C/G G | D7 D♯°7 Em |
Sudden - ly re - turn and nev - er,

C   G/D |D7   Gsus4 G |
Never-more Thy temples leave.

Em   B7|Em/B B |
Thee we would be always blessing,

G   C/G G |D/A A7 D   D7 |
Serve Thee as Thy hosts a - bove.

G   C/G G | D7 D♯°7 Em |
Pray and praise Thee with - out ceas - ing;

C   G/D |D7   G ||
Glory in Thy perfect love.

A Mighty Fortress Is Our God

Words and Music by Martin Luther
Translated by Frederick H. Hedge
Based on Psalm 46

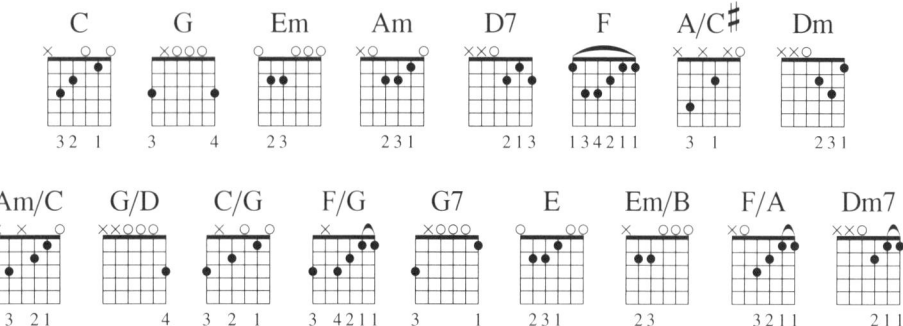

Verse 1

```
 ||C        G    Em |Am D7  G
  A mighty for - tress is   our God,
  Am|Em  F     C    A/C#|Dm G C
  A   bul - wark nev - er   fail - ing;
   |C        G    Em |Am D7  G
  Our helper He a - mid the flood
  Am|Em  F   C   A/C#|Dm G C
  Of  mor - tal ills pre - vail - ing.
   |C    Am/C G/D D7  |G
  For still our  an - cient foe
  C/G  |         F/G  G7|C
  Doth seek to work us  woe;
  E  |Am   Em/B Am/C D7 |G
  His craft and  pow'r are great,
  F   |         C/G F/A Dm|E
  And, armed with cru - el  hate,
  Am |Em   F C   A/C#|Dm7 G C
  On  earth is not his  e - qual.
```

Verse 2

```
‖C      G    Em │Am      D7   G
```
Did we in our own strength con - fide,
```
Am │Em   F   C      A/C♯│Dm G C
```
Our striv - ing would be   los - ing;
```
      │C      G    Em │Am D7  G
```
Were not the right Man on our side,
```
Am │Em   F   C      A/C♯│Dm   G   C
```
The Man of God's own   choos - ing:
```
      │C    Am/C G/D D7  │G
```
Dost ask who   that may be?
```
C/G   │        F/G G7│C
```
Christ Jesus, it   is He;
```
E    │Am   Em/B Am/C D7 │G
```
Lord Sab - a - oth, His Name,
```
F    │     C/G F/A Dm│E
```
From age to   age the same,
```
Am │Em F   C      A/C♯│Dm7 G  C
```
And He must win the   bat -   tle.

Verse 3

```
      ‖C          G    Em │Am  D7 G
```
And though this world, with dev - ils filled,
```
Am    │Em     F   C  A/C♯│Dm G C
```
Should threat - en to un - do   us,
```
      │C      G    Em│Am D7 G
```
We will not fear, for God hath willed
```
Am│Em   F   C   A/C♯ │Dm      G C
```
His truth to tri - umph through   us.
```
      │C      Am/C G/D   D7   │G
```
The Prince of   dark - ness grim,
```
C/G│           F/G G7 │C
```
We tremble not for him;
```
E   │Am   Em/B Am/C D7 │G
```
His rage we   can en - dure,
```
F   │   C/G F/A   Dm │E
```
For lo, his doom is   sure;
```
Am │Em F C      A/C♯│Dm7 G  C              ‖
```
One lit - tle word shall fell   him.

My Shepherd Will Supply My Need

Words by Isaac Watts
Paraphrased from Psalm 23
Music from Walker's Southern Harmony

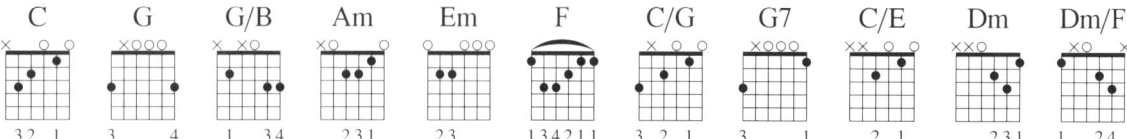

Verse 1

```
   ‖C    G   ‖C   G/B ‖Am G/B‖C
My Shep - herd will sup - ply my need;
Am ‖Em   F  ‖C/G G  G7‖C
Je - ho - vah is His    name.
   ‖C    G   ‖C   G/B ‖Am    G/B‖C
In pas - tures fresh He  makes me feed
Am‖Em   F  ‖C/G G  G7‖C
Be - side the liv - ing    stream.
G ‖C          ‖F   C/E ‖Dm  Dm/F ‖G
He brings my wan - d'ring spir - it    back
C    ‖Am Em‖F    Dm‖Am
When I   for - sake His ways,
   ‖C    G   ‖C   G/B‖Am  G/B‖C
And leads me, for His mer - cy's sake,
Am‖Em   F ‖C/G G  G7‖C
In   paths of truth and    grace.
```

Verse 2

```
      ‖C G   |C       G/B |Am     G/B |C
When I walk through the shades of  death,
Am|Em  F   |C/G G G7|C
Thy pres - ence is  my    stay.
      |C     G |C  G/B |Am   G/B |C
One word of Thy sup - port - ing  breath
Am    |Em F |C/G  G G7|C
Drives all my fears a - way.
G  |C          |F    C/E |Dm  Dm/F |G
Thy hand, in sight of  all   my    foes,
C    |Am  Em|F  Dm |Am
Doth still my ta - ble spread.
     |C  G  |C      G/B |Am G/B  |C
My cup with bless - ings o - ver - flows;
Am|Em F |C/G    G  G7|C
Thy oil a - noints my    head.
```

Verse 3

```
      ‖C    G   |C  G/B  |Am G/B|C
The sure pro - vi - sions of  my God
Am|Em  F  |C/G G G7|C
At - tend me all my    days.
     |C   G  |C       G/B |Am   G/B|C
O may Thy house be  mine a - bode
Am |Em F  |C/G   G  G7|C
And all my work be    praise!
G   |C         |F   C/E |Dm  Dm/F|G
There would I find a    set - tled  rest
C    |Am  Em|F  Dm |Am
While oth - ers go and come;
     |C    G |C      G/B |Am  G/B|C
No more a stran - ger, or   a    guest,
Am|Em  F|C/G   G  G7 |C                 ‖
But like a child at     home.
```

Nearer, My God, to Thee

Words by Sarah F. Adams
Based on Genesis 28:10-22
Music by Lowell Mason

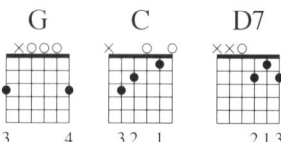

Verse 1

G |C |G |D7 |
Nearer, my God, to Thee, nearer to Thee!
G |C |G D7 |G |
E'en though it be a cross that raiseth me.
G C G | |
Still all my song shall be,
G   C G | D7 |
Near - er, my God, to Thee,
G |C |G D7 |G ||
Nearer, my God, to Thee, near - er to Thee!

Verse 2

G |C |G |D7 |
Though like the wanderer, the sun gone down,
G |C |G D7 |G |
Darkness be over me, my rest a stone.
G C G | |
Yet in my dreams I'd be,
G   C G | D7 |
Near - er, my God, to Thee,
G |C |G D7 |G ||
Nearer, my God, to Thee, near - er to Thee!

Verse 3

```
        G              |C              |G              |D7          |
Then,  with  my  waking  thoughts,  bright  with  Thy  praise,
        G        |C        |G   D7    |G          |
Out  of  my  stony  griefs  Be - thel  I'll  raise.
        G  C  G  |              |
So  by  my  woes  to  be,
        G    C  G  |        D7      |
Near - er,  my  God,  to  Thee,
        G        |C        |G    D7  |G              ||
Nearer,  my  God,  to  Thee,  near - er  to  Thee!
```

Verse 4

```
        G      |C        |G          |D7          |
Or  if  on  joyful  wing  cleaving  the  sky,
        G            |C          |G   D7    |G          |
Sun,  moon,  and  stars  forgot,  up - wards  I'll  fly.
        G  C  G  |              |
Still  all  my  song  shall  be,
        G    C  G  |        D7      |
Near - er,  my  God,  to  Thee,
        G        |C        |G    D7  |G              ||
Nearer,  my  God,  to  Thee,  near - er  to  Thee!
```

Now Thank We All Our God

German Words by Martin Rinkart
English Translation by Catherine Winkworth
Music by Johann Cruger

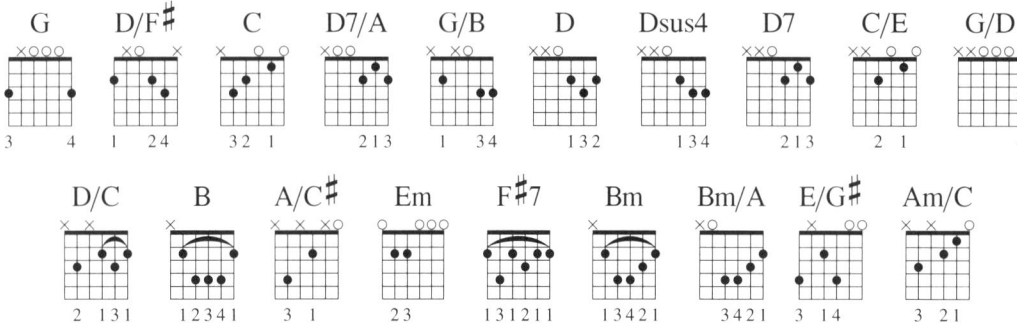

Verse 1

G ‖D/F# G C |G
Now thank we all our God,

　　|D7/A G/B D   G |Dsus4 D7 G
With heart and hands and voic - es,

　|G   C |G
Who wondrous things hath done,

　|C/E   G/D D/C   B |C D7 G
In whom His world re - joic - es;

D |A/C# D   G |D
Who from our mothers' arms

D/F#|G   D/F# Em F#7|Bm
Hath blessed us   on our way

Bm/A |E/G#   Am E/G#|Am
With   countless gifts of   love,

G/B |Am/C Em G/D   D |G
And still is   ours to - day.

Verse 2

```
        G‖D/F♯ G    C           |G
        O  may  this  bounteous  God
                |D7/A G/B  D    G |Dsus4  D7 G
        Through all    our  life  be  near      us,
             |G     C     |G
        With  ever-joyful  hearts
             |C/E    G/D  D/C    B |C      D7 G
        And  bless - ed   peace  to  cheer    us;
        D  |A/C♯  D  G       |D
        And  keep  us  in  His  grace,
        D/F♯ |G      D/F♯  Em     F♯7 |Bm
        And   guide us      when  per - plexed,
        Bm/A |E/G♯    Am    E/G♯ |Am
        And    free  us  from  all     ills
        G/B |Am/C Em      G/D  D  |G
        In   this   world  and  the  next.
```

Verse 3

```
        G ‖D/F♯   G   C          |G
        All  praise  and  thanks  to  God
             |D7/A  G/B  D     G |Dsus4  D7 G
        The  Fath - er   now  be  giv   -   en;
             |G         C          |G
        The  Son  and  Him  who  reigns
              |C/E    G/D  D/C    B |C      D7 G
        With  them  in   high - est  Heav  -  en;
        D  |A/C♯  D  G      |D
        The  one   e - ternal  God,
         D/F♯  |G      D/F♯  Em      F♯7 |Bm
        Whom  earth  and   Heav'n  a - dore;
        Bm/A |E/G♯    Am  E/G♯ |Am
        For    thus  it  was,  is     now,
        G/B |Am/C  Em  G/D  D |G                 ‖
        And  shall   be  ev - er - more.
```

O God, Our Help in Ages Past

Words by Isaac Watts
Music by William Croft

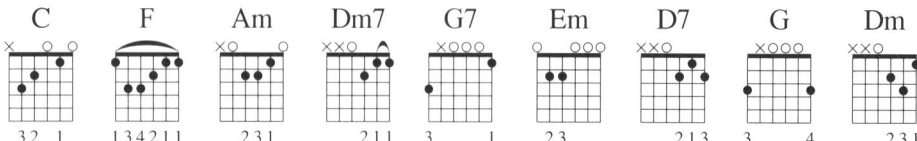

Verse 1

‖C   F   C   Am|Dm7 G7 C
O God, our help in ag - es past,

|Am Em F   D7|G
Our hope for years to come,

|C   F G7 |C   D7 G
Our shel - ter from the storm - y blast,

|F   C Dm G7|C
And our e - ter - nal home!

Verse 2

‖C   F   C   Am|Dm7 G7 C
Un - der the shad - ow of Thy throne,

|Am Em F   D7|G
Still may we dwell se - cure;

|C F   G7 |C   D7 G
Suf - fi - cient is Thine arm a - lone,

|F   C Dm G7|C
And our de - fense is sure

Verse 3

‖C   F   C   Am│Dm7 G7 C

Be - fore the hills in   or - der stood,

│Am   Em F   D7 │G

Or earth re - ceived her frame,

│C   F   G7   │C   D7 G

From ev - er - lasting, Thou art God,

│F   C   Dm   G7│C

To end - less years the same.

Verse 4

‖C   F   C   Am│Dm7 G7 C

A thou - sand ag - es, in   Thy sight,

│Am Em F   D7 │G

Are like an eve - ning gone;

│C F G7   │C   D7 G

Short as the watch that ends the night,

│F   C   Dm G7 │C   ‖

Be - fore the ris - ing sun.

O Master, Let Me Walk with Thee

Words by Washington Gladden
Music by H. Percy Smith

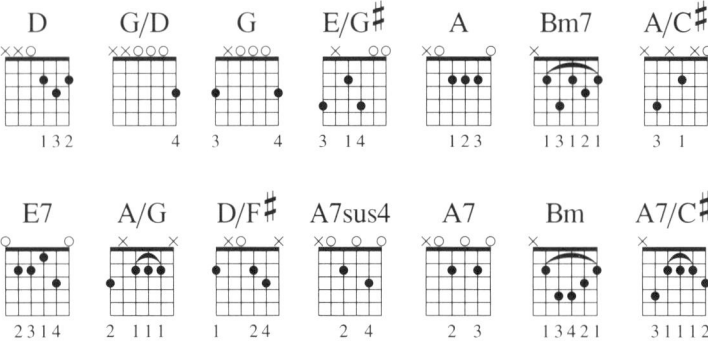

Verse 1

D |G/D D |G E/G♯|A |
O Master, let me walk with Thee

A Bm7 A/C♯|D   Bm7 |E7 |A |
In low - ly   paths of   service free.

A/G |D/F♯ |G   D/F♯|A7sus4 A7
Tell me Thy secret; help me   bear

D |A7   Bm |A7/C♯D |G   A |D ||
The strain of toil,   the fret of care.

Verse 2

D |G/D D |G E/G♯|A |
Help me the slow of heart to   move

A Bm7 A/C♯ |D   Bm7 |E7 |A |
By some clear, win - ning word of love.

A/G |D/F♯ |G   D/F♯|A7sus4 A7
Teach me the wayward feet to   stay,

D |A7   Bm |A7/C♯D |G   A |D ||
And guide them in   the home - ward way.

Verse 3

```
        D              |G/D D     |G    E/G♯|A              |
        Teach  me  Thy  pa - tience!  Still  with  Thee
        A  Bm7  A/C♯|D     Bm7 |E7      |A              |
        In  clos - er,  dear - er   compa - ny,
        A/G          |D/F♯        |G     D/F♯ |A7sus4  A7
        In  work  that  keeps  faith  sweet  and    strong,
        D  |A7   Bm |A7/C♯ D     |G   A  |D             ||
        In  trust  that  tri  -  umphs  o - ver  wrong.
```

Verse 4

```
        D              |G/D  D |G    E/G♯|A              |
        In  hope  that  sends  a  shin - ing    ray
        A   Bm7  A/C♯|D  Bm7 |E7        |A              |
        Far  down  the   fu - ture's  broad'ning  way,
        A/G          |D/F♯ |G    D/F♯ |A7sus4  A7
        In  peace  that  only     Thou  can'st  give,
        D   |A7   Bm|A7/C♯ D  |G   A  |D             ||
        With  Thee, O  Mas - ter,  let  me  live.
```

The Old Rugged Cross

Words and Music by
Rev. George Bennard

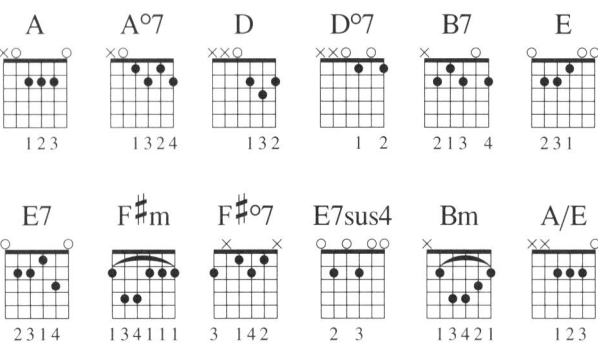

Verse 1

||A   A°7|A |D   D°7|D
On a hill far a - way stood an old rug - ged cross,

B7 |E |E7 |A |F♯m
The emblem of suffering and shame;

E7 |A   A°7|A |D   D°7|D
And I love that old cross, where the dearest and best

B7 |E |E7 |A |
For a world of lost sinners was slain.

Refrain

F♯°7 ||E7 | |A |
So I'll cherish the old rugged cross

    |D | |A |
Till my trophies at last I lay down;

E7sus4|A | |D |Bm
I will cling to the old rugged cross

    |A/E |E7 |A |
And ex - change it some day for a crown.

Verse 2

```
      ‖A         A°7|A              |D        D°7|D
```
To the old rug - ged cross I will ever be   true,
```
B7 |E              |E7           |A            |F♯m
```
It's shame and re - proach gladly bear;
```
E7        |A       A°7 |A          |D           D°7|D
```
Then He'll call me some day to my home far a - way,
```
B7         |E         |E7       |A            |
```
Where His glory for - ever I'll share.

Refrain

```
F♯°7  ‖E7           |             |A          |
```
So I'll cherish the old rugged cross
```
         |D           |         |A           |
```
Till my trophies at last I lay down;
```
E7sus4|A           |          |D          |Bm
```
I will   cling to the old rugged cross
```
      |A/E          |E7       |A           |            ‖
```
And ex - change it some day for a crown.

Onward, Christian Soldiers

Words by Sabine Baring-Gould
Music by Arthur S. Sullivan

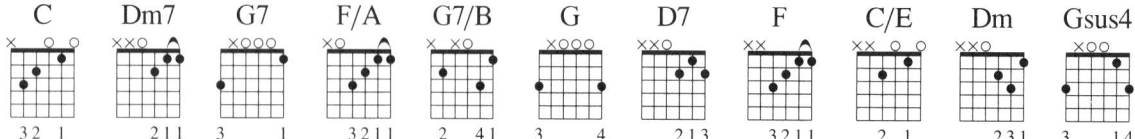

Verse 1

C   **|Dm7 G7**   **|**
Onward, Christian sol - diers,

G7   **F/A G7/B** **|C**   **|**
Marching as to war,

C   **|Dm7 G**   **|**
With the cross of Je - sus

D7   **|G**   **|**
Going on be - fore!

G   **|C**   **|**
Christ, the royal Master,

C   **|F**   **|**
Leads against the foe.

F   **C/E**   **Dm C/E** **|F** **C/E Dm C/E|**
For - ward in - to bat - tle,

F **C/E Dm C** **|G**   **||**
See His ban - ners go!

Refrain

C   **|Dm7 G7**   **|**
Onward, Christian sol - diers,

G7   **|C**   **|**
Marching as to war,

C   **Dm7**   **|C/E C**   **|**
With the cross of Je - sus

F   **Gsus4 G** **|C**   **||**
Going on   be - fore!

Verse 2

C |Dm7 G7 |
Like a mighty ar - my

G7   F/A   G7/B |C |
Moves the church of   God.

C |Dm7   G |
Brothers, we are tread - ing

D7 |G |
Where the saints have trod.

G |C |
We are not di - vided,

C |F |
All one body, we,

F   C/E Dm   C/E |F   C/E Dm C/E |
One in   hope and doc - trine,

F   C/E Dm   C |G   ‖
One in   char - i - ty.

Repeat Refrain

Verse 3

C |Dm7   G7 |
Onward, then, ye peo - ple,

G7   F/A G7/B |C |
Join our hap - py   throng.

C |Dm7   G |
Blend with ours your voic - es

D7 |G |
In the triumph song.

G |C |
Glory, laud, and hon - or

C |F |
Unto Christ the King.

F   C/E   Dm   C/E |F C/E Dm C/E |
This through count - less a - ges

F   C/E Dm C |G   ‖
Men and an - gels sing.

Repeat Refrain

Praise to the Lord, the Almighty

Words by Joachim Neander
Translated by Catherine Winkworth
Music from Erneuerten Gesangbuch

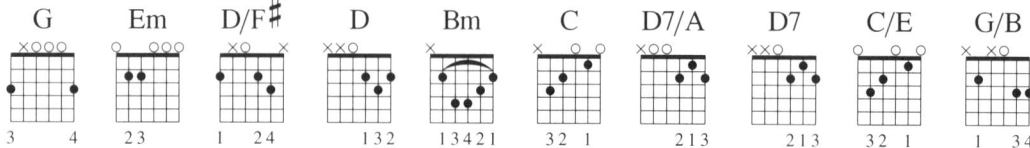

Verse 1

```
G      Em D/F♯|G
Praise to  the  Lord,

D   Em|Bm    C
The Al - might - y,

G    |C    D7/A Em |C  D D7|G            |
The King of   cre - a   -   tion!

G Em D/F♯|G     D
O  my soul, praise Him,

Em|Bm C G |C       D7/A Em |C  D D7 |G         |
For he  is thy health and  sal - va   -   tion!

G  D/F♯G  |C           |
All ye   who hear,

G   C/E D/F♯|G    D7/A G  |D          |
Now to  His  tem - ple  draw near,

G/B  C  D7/A|Em  C  Bm |C  D D7|G          ||
Join - ing in    glad ad - o - ra   -   tion.
```

Verse 2

G   Em D/F♯|G
Praise to the Lord,

D   Em |Bm C
Who o'er all things

G |C   D7/A Em|C   D D7|G |
So wond - rous - ly reign   - eth,

G   Em D/F♯|G D   Em|Bm   C
Shelt - ers thee un - der his wings, yea,

G |C   D7/A Em |C D D7 |G |
So gen - tly   sus - tain   - eth!

G   D/F♯ G |C |
Hast thou not seen?

G C/E D/F♯|G   D7/A G |D |
All that is   need - ful   hath been

G/B   C D7/A|Em C Bm |C   D D7 |G   ‖
Grant - ed in   what He or - dain   - eth.

Rock of Ages

Words by Augustus M. Toplady
V.1,2 altered by Thomas Cotterill
Music by Thomas Hastings

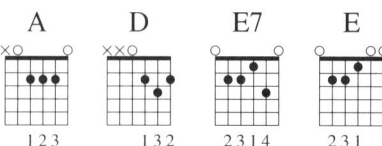

Verse 1

‖A   D |A
Rock of Ages, cleft for me,
E7 |A   E7 |A
Let me hide my - self in Thee;
|E |A
Let the water and the blood,
|E |A
From Thy wounded side which flowed,
|A   D |A
Be of sin the double cure;
D |A   E7 |A
Save from wrath and make me pure.

Verse 2

‖A   D |A
Could my tears for - ever flow,
E7 |A   E7 |A
Could my zeal no languor know;
|E |A
These for sin could not a - tone,
|E |A
Thou must save and Thou a - lone;
|A   D |A
In my hand no price I bring,
D |A   E7 |A
Simply to Thy cross I cling.

Verse 3

    ‖**A**   **D** |**A**
While I draw this fleeting breath,

E7 |**A**   **E7** |**A**
When my eyes shall close in death,

     |**E** |**A**
When I rise to worlds un - known,

     |**E** |**A**
And be - hold Thee on Thy throne,

    |**A** **D** |**A**
Rock of Ages, cleft for me,

D |**A**   **E7** |**A**   ‖
Let me hide my - self in Thee.

Shall We Gather at the River?

Words and Music by
Robert Lowry

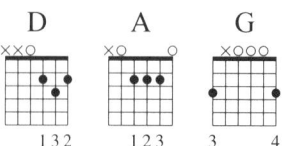

Verse 1

D | |
Shall we gather at the river,
A | |
Where bright angel feet have trod,
D |
With its crystal tide for - ever
|**A** |**D** ||
Flowing from the throne of God?

Refrain

G |**D**
Yes, we'll gather at the river,
|**A** |**D** |
The beautiful, the beautiful river;
G |**D**
Gather with the saints at the river
|**A** |**D** ||
That flows from the throne of God.

Verse 2

D | |
On the margin of the river,
A | |
Washing up its silver spray,
D |
We will walk and worship ever,
    |A |D ||
All the happy golden day.

Repeat Refrain

Verse 3

D | |
On the bosom of the river,
A | |
Where the Savior King we own,
D |
We shall meet and sorrow never
    |A |D ||
'Neath the glory of the throne.

Repeat Refrain

Softly and Tenderly

Words and Music by
Will L. Thompson

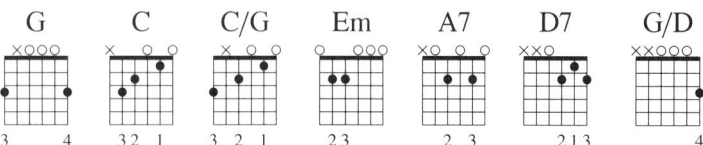

Verse 1

G | |**C** |**C/G** **G** |
Softly and tenderly Jesus is call - ing,
G |**Em** |**A7** |**D7** |
Calling for you and for me.
G | |**C** |**C/G** **G** |
See, on the portals He's waiting and watch - ing,
G **C** |**G/D** **D7** |**G** **C** |**G**
Watching for you and for me.

Refrain

||**D7** | |**G/D** **D7** |**G/D** |
Come home, come home;
A7 | |**D** |**D7** |
You who are weary, come home.
G | |**C** |**C/G** **G** |
Earnestly, tenderly, Jesus is call - ing,
G **C** |**G/D** **D7** |**G** **C** |**G** ||
Calling, O sinner, come home.

Verse 2

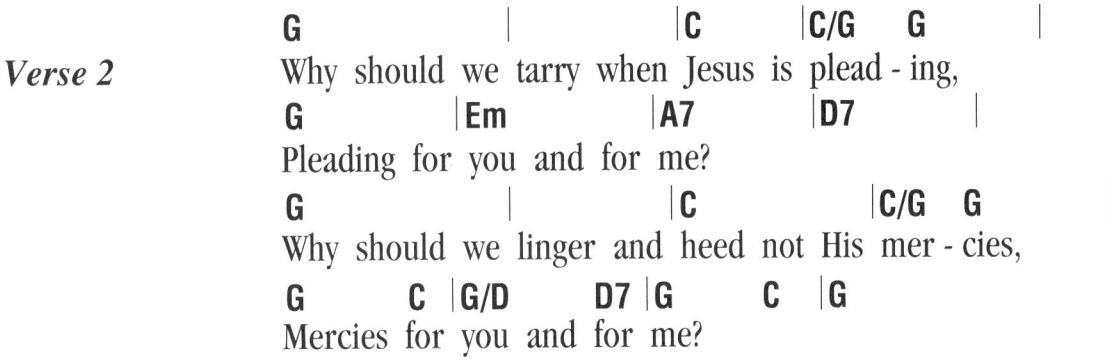

```
G                        |C         |C/G   G        |
Why should we tarry when Jesus is plead - ing,
G        |Em       |A7        |D7              |
Pleading for you and for me?
G                        |C           |C/G   G            |
Why should we linger and heed not His mer - cies,
G      C |G/D      D7 |G        C  |G
Mercies for you and for me?
```

Repeat Refrain

Verse 3

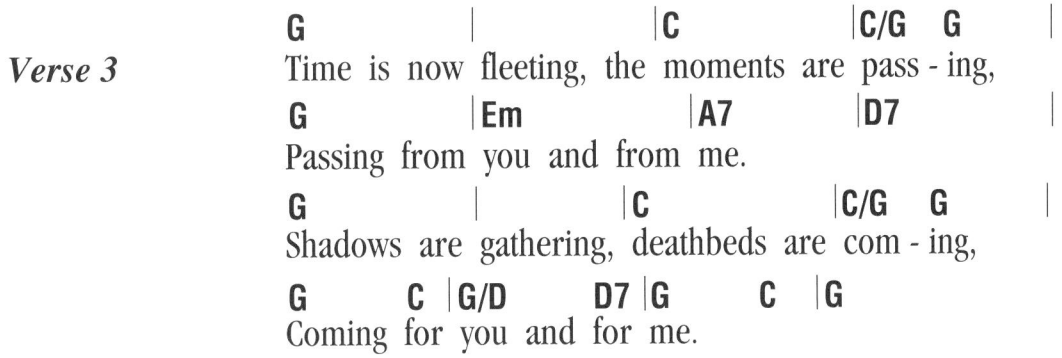

```
G                        |C           |C/G   G        |
Time is now fleeting, the moments are pass - ing,
G        |Em       |A7        |D7              |
Passing from you and from me.
G                |C           |C/G   G        |
Shadows are gathering, deathbeds are com - ing,
G      C |G/D      D7 |G        C  |G
Coming for you and for me.
```

Repeat Refrain

We Gather Together

Words from Nederlandtsch Gedenckclanck
Translated by Theodore Baker
Netherlands Folk Melody

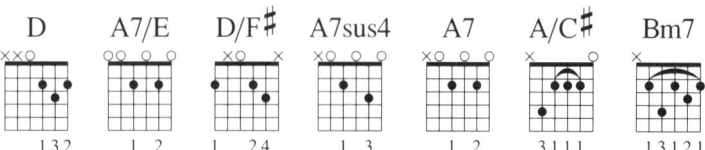

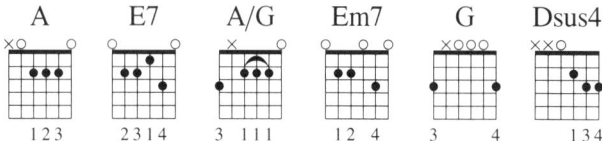

Verse 1

|D | A7/E D/F# |A7sus4 A7 |D
We gather to - geth - er to ask the Lord's blessing;

|A/C# |Bm7 A |E7 |A
He chastens and hastens His will to make known.

|A/G |D/F# |Em7 A7 |D
The wicked op - pressing now cease from dis - tressing.

|G |D/F# Bm7 |Em7 A7sus4 A7 |D
Sing praises to His Name; He for - gets not His own.

Verse 2

‖D | A7/E D/F# |A7sus4 A7|D
Be - side us to guide us, our God with us joining,

|A/C# |Bm7 A |E7 |A
Or - daining, main - taining His kingdom di - vine;

|A/G |D/F# |Em7 A7 |D
So from the be - ginning the fight we were winning;

|G |D/F# Bm7|Em7 A7sus4 A7 |D
Thou, Lord, wast at our side; all glo - ry be Thine!

Verse 3

```
       ‖D              |        A7/E   D/F♯ |A7sus4 A7 |D
```
We all do ex - tol Thee, Thou Leader tri - umphant,
```
       |A/C♯            |Bm7       A  |E7           |A
```
And pray that Thou still our De - fender will be.
```
       |A/G            |D/F♯         |Em7  A7   |D
```
Let Thy congre - gation es - cape tribu - lation;
```
       |G              |D/F♯      Bm7|Em7  A7sus4 A7  |D            ‖
```
Thy name be ever praised! O   Lord, make   us free!

When I Survey the Wondrous Cross

Words by Isaac Watts
Music arranged by Lowell Mason
Based on Plainsong

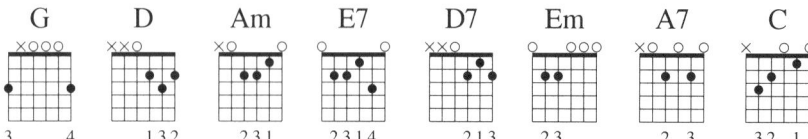

G   D   Am   E7   D7   Em   A7   C

Verse 1

```
       G        D |G   AmE7|Am  G    D |G            |
       When I sur-vey the    won-drous     cross
       G            |D7      |G   D7Em|A7      D7     |
       On which the Prince of glo-ry       died,
       G        D |G   AmE7|Am  G   D |G            |
       My rich-est gain I      count but   loss,
       G            |D7   Em|Am D7|G            ||
       And pour con-tempt on all my pride.
```

Verse 2

```
       G     D |G    AmE7|Am  G    D |G            |
       Forbid it, Lord, that I    should   boast,
       G            |D7      |G   D7Em|A7     D7     |
       Save in the death of Christ my    Lord!
       G     D |G   AmE7|Am   G D |G            |
       All the vain things that  charm me    most,
       G        |D7  Em  |Am D7|G            ||
       I sacri-fice them to His blood.
```

Verse 3

```
    G        D  |G     Am E7|Am    G   D |G          |
See, from His head, His    hands, His    feet,
    G          |D7      |G   D7 Em|A7      D7      |
Sorrow and love flow min - gled    down!
    G        D |G    Am E7|Am G  D |G              |
Did e'er such love and    sor - row  meet,
    G          |D7   Em |Am  D7|G              ||
Or thorns com - pose so   rich a   crown?
```

Verse 4

```
    G        D  |G     Am E7|Am G  D |G              |
Were the whole realm of     na - ture  mine,
    G          |D7      |G  D7 Em|A7       D7      |
That were a present far too    small;
    G       D |G    Am E7|Am G  D |G              |
Love so a - maz - ing,    so di - vine,
    G          |D7   Em|Am  D7|G              ||
Demands my soul, my life, my all.
```

Simple Gifts

Traditional Shaker Hymn

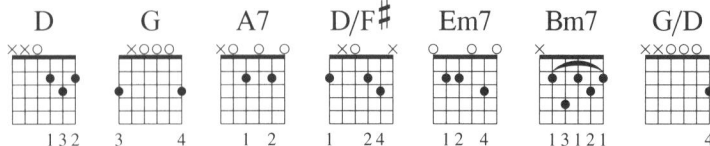

Verse 1

|D |
'Tis the gift to be simple, 'tis the gift to be free,
|G |A7
'Tis the gift to come down where you ought to be,
|D |
And when we find ourselves in the place just right,
|G | D ||
'Twill be in the valley of love and de - light.

Refrain

D |G   D/F♯ Em7
When true sim - plici - ty is gained,
|D   Bm7 |Em7   A7
To bow and to bend we won't be a - shamed.
|D   G/D |D
To turn, turn will be our delight
|G   A7 |G/D   D ||
Till by turning and turning we come out right.